Textual Non Sense

Textual Non Sense

A Four-Part Trilogy

by Robert Crawford

Beyond Criticism Editions

BOILER HOUSE PRESS

Le non sens est la chose du monde la mieux partagée
– Descartes

For N. M.,
Profreader

Contents

Acknowledgements

In addition to thanking my wife for lying about this book while I was writing it, I extend my deep gratitude to the two anonymous readers, Professor M. T. Trasch of Digital University and Professor U. Conn of Yukon College, whose many suggestions I hope to incorporate into the second volume. Thanks are due, also, to John Haddock for alerting me to the Haddock Prize for works which mention that noble fish. Sadly, my old friend and loyal proofreader, Nigel Migraine, died almost halfway through the first proofs, and I dedicate this work to his memry.

PART ONE

Introduction, Preface and Prolegomenon

Operating in the zone of unstable convergences between post-haptic theory and cognitive neuroscience, 'textual non sense' presents a vertiginously disruptive challenge to the verbal semiotic; omnipresent, yet always elusive, it operates as an insistent uncertainty principle, an aporia at the very heart of written discourse, meaning that meaning at any moment both is and, simultaneously, is not.

Roland Butter

Humour and literary criticism go together like apples and arsenic.[1] Humour and creative writing, however, have danced hand-in-hand from Aristophanes to Old Possum and beyond. Though the tragic is so often seen as much more deserving of attention than the comic, everyone can name comic poets, novelists, and dramatists; no one can name a comic literary critic.

In the institutions of the English-speaking world, as part of what has been called 'the Scottish Invention of English Literature', university classes in vernacular literature were first taught by Adam Smith, a thinker most often associated with what Thomas Carlyle later termed 'the *dismal science*' of economics.[2] At Glasgow University in the 1750s, Smith's class on 'Rhetoric and Belles Lettres' was not wholeheartedly dismal, and attracted some notable students including the future biographer James Boswell; but it is hard to

---

1 This part of the book will have lots of footnotes; but don't worry, none of the other parts will have any at all. In line with modern academic practice, I have cited as many of my own publications as possible. Lord or Lady X, one of the anonymous peers who shrewdly reviewed my typescript, points out that those two works of Frederick Crews, *The Pooh Perplex* (1963; 2nd ed., Chicago: University of Chicago Press, 2003) and *Postmodern Pooh* (Evanston: Northwestern University Press, 2006) are exceptions that prove the rule about humour and literary criticism. Oscar Wilde's brilliant dialogue 'The Critic as Artist' is just too clotted with profundities to count.

2 See Robert Crawford, *Devolving English Literature*, 2nd ed. (Edinburgh: Edinburgh University Press, 2000), Chapter 1; and Robert Crawford, ed., *The Scottish Invention of English Literature* (Cambridge: Cambridge University Press, 1998); see Thomas Carlyle's scandalously racist essay 'Occasional Discourse on the Nigger Question', reprinted in his *Critical and Miscellaneous Essays* (London: Chapman and Hall, 1903), 8 vols., VII, 84.

find any jokes in the surviving lecture notes.[3] Smith was interested in kinds of exchange – sympathetic, verbal, and economic; for him these were hardly laughing matters. Nor were they a source of merriment for his fellow teachers of Rhetoric and Belles Lettres, who included the Reverend Dr Hugh Blair at the University of Edinburgh. An upstanding Kirk minister renowned for his somewhat bland 'Moderate' sermons, Blair became the first Anglophone academic in the world to hold the title Professor of Rhetoric and Belles Lettres. His contemporary Professor William Barron, successor to the rhetorical professor Robert Watson at the University of St Andrews, had interests in culture that encompassed not just literary culture but also agriculture: at an ancient university, several of whose professors owned local farms, Barron wrote a book about ploughs. Hesiod and Virgil might have understood such a world-view that saw culture and ploughing as one, but it took the 'ploughman poet' Robert Burns to connect both of these with subversive and revealing humour; the rather barren academic Barron never managed it in any of his dusty writings. While the professors of Rhetoric and Belles Lettres lectured, their students borrowed from the university library books such as the hilarious comedies of Molière and the rollicking

---

3   Adam Smith, *Lectures on Rhetoric and Belles Lettres*, ed. J. C. Bryce (Oxford: Clarendon Press, 1983); Boswell recalled how 'Dr Adam Smith, in his rhetorical lectures at Glasgow, told us he was glad to know that Milton wore latchets in his shoes, instead of buckles' – just the sort of detail that writers treasure, though it may also have been as close as Smith ever got to a joke. See James Boswell, *The Journal of a Tour to the Hebrides*, ed. R. W. Chapman (1924; repr. Oxford: Oxford University Press, 1974), 171.

picaresque novels of Tobias Smollett.[4] Probably the first significant poet to encounter Rhetoric and Belles Lettres as a university student was the young Robert Fergusson in the 1760s, who got his revenge on his *alma mater* and on his teachers in his satirical Scots poem 'To the Principal and Professors of the University of St Andrews, on their Superb Treat to Samuel Johnson.' With comic brio Fergusson delivers a mock-lecture to the academics, and is clearly embarrassed by their sycophancy to the supposed Grand Arbiter of English literary and linguistic taste.[5]

While no one can name a comic literary critic, it might just be possible to argue that Alexander Pope in his 'Essay on Criticism' is the exception that proves this rule. Pope's take on criticism is characteristically and nimbly elegant, as well as still quotable:

> True Wit is *Nature* to Advantage drest,
> What oft was *Thought*, but ne'er so well *Exprest*[6]

but many modern readers find even Pope's 744 lines of literary criticism and literary history *de trop*. For most of us,

---

4   Eighteenth-century students' library borrowings (and the library borrowings of professors) were recorded in ledgers, and some of these can be viewed online among the Digital Collections of the University of St Andrews.

5   Fergusson's poem is reprinted in Robert Crawford and Mick Imlah, ed., *The Penguin Book* of Scottish Verse (London: Penguin Classics, 2006), 274-276.

6   Alexander Pope, *The Poems*, ed. John Butt (London: Methuen, 1965), 153.

as for Polonius in *Hamlet*, 'brevity is the soul of wit.'[7]

If Pope still makes readers smile, though, it is because he is more of a poet than a critic: his elegant view of criticism is balletic, rather than academic, and he knows better than any other poet in English how the pauses marked by poetic punctuation, caesurae and enjambments are vital to sense and to the senses; this is what leads to his witty dancing, his laughter. Popeian possibilities were closed down by some of Pope's admirers: is there a more humourless poet in English than William Wordsworth? You could try reading through Coleridge's voluminous writings in search of a credible joke, but few would advise it. Byron, in *English Bards and Scotch Reviewers* and elsewhere, may carry a Popeian torch, but as the nineteenth century advances, that torch gutters and is snuffed out. Thanks to Edward Lear and several other authors the Victorian age produced wonderful, sometimes vertiginously balanced nonsense verse, but no notable nonsense criticism.

What snuffs out the torch is the growing institutionalization of academic Eng Lit. After the moment when, in the mid-nineteenth century, London University catches the Rhetoric and Belles Lettres bug (which, by that time, had already infected America and India), the old English elite universities of Oxford and Cambridge begin, towards the end of the century, to wake up to studying English literary texts through the medium of the English language. The

---

7   William Shakespeare, *Hamlet*, II, ii, 97.

bewhiskered Professor of Poetry Matthew Arnold is often conjured up in this context, but the author of *Culture and Anarchy, Essays in Criticism*, etc., etc., etc., is never invoked for his lightheartedness. The post-Arnoldian incarceration of Eng Lit within high, sometimes unscalable academic walls is a dour tale, albeit one told with gusto and wit by Stephen Potter in *The Muse in Chains*.[8]

Perhaps because it was seen by some as frivolously feminine in comparison with the manly, imperial subject of Classics, twentieth-century Eng Lit and Crit tried so hard to be po-faced, but did so in an unArnoldian, clean-shaven, thoroughly modern way. Ivor Armstrong Richards set out English Lit Crit in his *Practical Criticism* as if it was fit in every way for a scientific textbook: Richards removed the titles from poems and called them coldly 'Poem I', 'Poem II', and 'Poem XII'; students too were changed from names to numbers: '12.23 ... 12.24 ... 12.25'.[9] Cambridge and Harvard (at both of which Richards held appointments) adored this lab-coated way of doing things, and the New Criticism became à la mode. For all that he was a poet who was booted out of Cambridge, Richards's admirer the future professor William Empson extended criticism-by-numbers as far as it would stretch on the Procrustean rack of his *Seven Types of Ambiguity*. In the hands of such men (and occasionally women), English Studies became respectable as a form of

---

8   Stephen Potter, *The Muse in Chains* (London: Methuen, 1937).

9   I. A. Richards, *Practical Criticism: A Study of Literary Judgment* (1929; rpt. London: Routledge, 1978), ix, 12, 156.

torture, a meticulous Gradgrindian exam mill mocked by the poet Auden in his own spoof *English Study, The Orators*, where 'Candidates must write on three sides of the paper.'[10] The fight for status and respectability made the seriousness of the subject all the more essential. Criticism – whether quasi-scientific, moralising, philological, or vestigially belles-lettristic -- needed maximal gravitas. Leavis and levity simply didn't mix.

A mid-twentieth-century backlash of campus novels by Kingsley Amis, Vladimir Nabokov, Malcolm Bradbury and others mocked academic grandiosity; but this had the unintended effect of reinforcing many academics' own sense of their pursuit of High Seriousness; or else it led to a certain sort of pass-the-port donnish wit that was fine for the glinting silverware of Oxbridge High Tables but rarely made it on to the page in a way that would actually make anyone laugh. Academia was a calling, not a cat-call -- a job, after all, not a joke. In the wake of World War II the growth of the university sector throughout the English-speaking world and an increasing awareness of continental European literary theory, despite various outbreaks of news-worthy wrangling, kept on failing to amuse. There were bad boys and bad girls of criticism – iconoclasts from Jacques Derrida to Hélène Cixous – but they showed a marked preference for abjection or différance or archive fever over anything that could be called a giggle. The business of criticism, not least

---

10   W. H. Auden, *The English Auden*, ed. Edward Mendelson (London: Faber and Faber, 1977), 92.

when it became six-figure remunerative in Paris or California, was a Serious Business: closer to masturbation in public than to merriment, the *jouissance* of Roland Barthes is hardly jokiness; in private, Barthes wrote his *Mourning Diary* rather than collecting quips.[11]

Deconstruction, which might have done much to unpick professorial pomposity, instead reinforced it, giving scholars from Yale to Yerevan yet more nuggets of arcane, hierarchical language which might seal them off from the vulgar world. Even when the Russian theorist Mikhail Bakhtin's theories of the carnivalesque reached the West, it was reassuring to serious-minded critics that no prose was more ponderous than that of this po-faced, brilliant analyst of topsyturvydom. Though Jürgen Habermas, it must be said, has vied with Bakhtin in solemnity.

There may, from time to time, have been attempts to disrupt academic hyper-gravitas. Drawing on students' wit and witlessness, poet and Glasgow University Eng Lit professor Edwin Morgan published his 'Hantle of Howlers' with its 'More's Uptopia', and 'Shakespierre'; critic, editor and Oxford University professor John Carey published an essay called 'Down with Dons'; more recently, John Schad and Oliver Tearle (critics and creative writers both) assembled a distinguished and provocatively mutinous crew in their co-edited *Crrritic!* whose rambunctious subtitle,

---

11 *Mourning Diary* is the English title of Roland Barthes' *Journal de Deuil*, and was translated by Richard Howard (London: Notting Hill Editions, 2011).

Sighs, Cries, Lies, Insults, Outbursts, Hoaxes, Disasters, Letters of Resignation, and Various Other Noises Off in These the First and Last Days of Literary Criticism ... Not to Mention the University comes closer than anything else to the spirit of the present book.[12] Overall, however, sadly little changed when it came to the assumption that literary criticism required its own immensely serious procedures. Feminism and queer theory, productively disruptive but seldom side-splitting, may have called attention to the spare rib and a poetics of transgression, but most feminists saw the stakes as far too high to snigger. Judith Butler is no court jester.

What ought to have changed criticism for the better was the advent of the teaching of Creative Writing – which swept in a blizzard of foolscap across American campuses in the early and mid-twentieth century -- though one can argue that it had long been taught in ancient Greece through *progymnasmata*, in Shakespeare's England through forms of Renaissance schooling, and in universities in Scotland and elsewhere as part of Rhetoric and Belles Lettres since the eighteenth century.[13] Whatever its antecedents, however, Creative Writing became the most significant new area in British English departments in the later part of the

---

12 Edwin Morgan, 'A Hantle of Howlers', in *Essays* (Cheadle Hulme: Carcanet, 1974), 259, 269; John Carey, 'Down with Dons', *The New Review*, I, 10 (1975); John Schad and Oliver Teale, ed., *Crrritic!* (Brighton: Sussex Academic Press, 2011).

13 See Neil Rhodes, *Shakespeare and the Origins of English* (Oxford: Oxford University Press, 2004), especially Chapter 2, 'Did Shakespeare Study Creative Writing?'

twentieth century. Poets', dramatists' and novelists' publications were devoured by many a government-sponsored Research Assessment Exercise or Research Excellence Framework, and the jingle of Creative Writing students' fees helped fill university coffers. Financially, Creative Writing was a bonanza for poets too. Yet in America, Canada and Britain Creative Writing, rather than frolicking, often found itself in a wary stand-off with academic lit crit. 'CW' chose to institutionalize itself and get itself taken seriously by mustering as much solemnity as its many proponents could muster.

There were some gales of laughter. When the artist, novelist, poet and dramatist Alasdair Gray briefly taught Creative Writing in the School of English at the University of St Andrews in the 1990s, Castle House (a.k.a. The Poetry House) shook with his high-pitched guffaws. Possibly he laughed more at his own jokes than the students did, but that was a risk worth taking. Generally, though, Creative Writers, anxious to be regarded seriously in their own institutions, have tried to cultivate a po-faced front as members of the English Department; or else they have got themselves kicked out of English departments, usually after a fissiparous tussle between critics and creatives that left the critics to concentrate (seriously) on lit crit in their own enclave, and the writers to focus (also seriously) on creative writing in theirs. A few writers, of course, have got themselves kicked out altogether – but seldom for their sense of humour.

Humour is an essential corrective that needs to be introduced – perhaps avid fans of Pope would say 'reintroduced' – into both criticism and the teaching of creative writing if these are to maintain contact with a wider public. Literature doesn't just belong to universities. Many academics want to write only for their peers – sometimes a very limited circle – and are happy to publish on so-called 'open access' sites where their work is read solely by search engines and fellow academic researchers. Too often 'open access' publishing goes hand in hand with writing for a closed scholarly ghetto: the Borg writing for the Borg.[14] Ways out of that ghetto include the writing of biography and some kinds of cultural and literary history. Another way out of the ghetto is to laugh yourself out, because laughter is something shared, something that can produce widespread communal glee, rather than simply a solitary or a ghetto pleasure.

The work offered in *Textual Non Sense* is mischievous and minimalist. In the spirit of the deliciously bookish ancient Greek poet Callimachus, the prevailing assumption is that less is more. Nimbleness and elegance, fun and frolics are forms of release: liberation from the droning boredom of too many a classroom into a zone of smiles. To critics in universities, artists in universities, and creative writers in universities this volume offers entertainment that may afford at times a liberating potential. But this book ain't only for people immured in academe. Perhaps, too, it may lead to common perceptions inside and outside universities of

---

14 This is an allusion to *Star Trek*.

just what it is about particular literary jokes and tropes that provokes the instant recognition which accompanies wit and grinning. If you never laugh out loud when you read what follows, I'll be sorry; but I do recognize that much of what's here is a lot closer to wit than it is to stand-up. So, wary reader, be assured that a smile will suffice.

Luis Henrique Boaventura and Ernani Cesar de Freitas in their 2014 article 'Style as a Bonding Element between Stand-up Comedy and Literature' are very, very rare in their desire to relate comedy to criticism, but I fear that their research, which they describe dutifully as 'descriptive and bibliographic with a qualitative approach', risks killing the jokes they so evidently relish.[15] The aim of *Textual Non Sense* is not to put any jokes to the sword, but to encourage readers to make more of their own: to set loose a spirit of laughter, repartee and wit among the groaning library stacks of English, Literary Criticism, Creative Writing, Typographical Science, Cultural Studies, Semiotics, Digital Humanities, and other subjects too. There may be no belly-laughs in this book, but it does aim to be fun.

Can threats to the Arts and Humanities be laughed off? I hope so. Certainly, laughter may be a defence at least as good as any turgid report on the value of the humanities. It may be good to laugh in the cannon's mouth, as well as in (and with) the mouth of the canon. For through humour

---

15 Luis Henrique Boaventura and Ernani Cesar de Freitas, 'Style as a Bonding Element between Stand-up Comedy and Literature', *Intercom: Revista Brasiliera de Ciências da Comunicação*, 37.2 (July/December 2014), Introduction.

people across a surprising range of countries in Europe, North America, and further afield can come to realise that, even though many folk think they live in a post-literate era, more audiences around the world enjoy – and even study – literary texts than ever before, and can 'message' about them in ways that are readily comprehensible. In our age when there are more texts on phones than in libraries, our texts, while (like so many Classical fragments) being among the shortest of memes, may send the message that a literary heritage still connects diverse communities, and that, comically perhaps, literary texts, literary 'texts', and texts and 'texts' about literature remain a way to reach not just a pan-European population but a global audience beyond. I'd like to imagine out there among my readers not just students of the graphic arts as well as the literary arts, but also a range of adults and children, and even the ghost of that African Classicist, teacher, and poet of 'the sky in monocle', Christopher Okigbo.[16] As Okigbo knew only too well, Classics lies at the root of so much Anglophone poetry; moreover, whether fused with all sorts of other materials or taken straight like a single malt, it still packs a lingering and surprisingly lovable punch. To stand up for the Arts and Humanities does not always require a stand-up, bareknuckle fight; sometimes the most effective way is to let folk drink straight from the Pierian Spring.[17]

---

16   Christopher Okigbo, *Labyrinths* (London: Heinemann, 1971), 13.

17   It may be only fair to point out that Alexander Pope in 'An Essay on Criticism' advises, 'A *little Learning* is a dang'rous Thing;/ Drink deep, or taste not the Pierian Spring' (Pope, op. cit., 151).

Coming from the Brasilian-influenced Scottish culture that produced both the concrete poems of Edwin Morgan and the Classically-inflected visual poems of Ian Hamilton Finlay, the use of texts in this book also emerges from my own earlier work making Scots and English versions of Greek and Latin poems by poets from Sappho and Simonides to George Buchanan and Arthur Johnston; but it derives, too, from working with the photographer Norman McBeath on several collaborations that have produced what the critic Michael Nott terms, in his 2018 history of the topic, 'photopoetry'; and from working with the typographer Robert Dalrymple who designs many of the publications of Norman McBeath's Easel Press and of the National Galleries of Scotland. [18]

Can a verbal icon, a one-word poem, or a similarly fragment-sized textual utterance have as immediate effect as a photograph or any other example of visual art? Well, we'll see. Collaborating with visual artists has made me keen to explore ways in which verbal art could fuse with visual art, becoming instantaneously graphic. Also, producing several solemn collaborations, and serving in 2016 for a wonderful brief stint as President of the Classical Association (an experience which intensified a fascination with the fragment as a telling literary form) made me long for something lighter

---

18   See, e.g., Robert Crawford, *Full Volume* (London: Cape, 2008), 33; Robert Crawford, ed. and trans., *Apollos of the North: Selected Poems of George Buchanan and Arthur Johnston* (Edinburgh: Polygon, 2006); Robert Crawford, *Simonides*, with photographs by Norman McBeath (Edinburgh: Easel Press, 2011); Michael Nott, *Photopoetry: A History* (New York: Bloomsbury, 2018); for Robert Dalrymple's designs for Easel Press, see https://www.normanmcbeath. com/about-easel-press

and more mischievous.[19] The text-work of this book (which is in four parts, of which this is the first) may have one foot in pedagogy, but it waves the other foot about in the air as balletically as it can, and would love to leap like Nijinsky.

Part two of this volume is *Writers' Struggles: A Text Book*. Formally, it shows how texting offers textuality a re-energized sense of play. *Writers' Struggles* deals too, of course, with much grimmer matter, and emerges from years of teaching Creative Writing in many a worthy workshop. Creative Writing as a discipline has produced a proliferation of 'aims and objectives' or 'how to' guides over the last few decades, and spawned a whole industry of professional sludge.[20] The best theoretical writing to emerge from this area, including most notably that of Don Paterson, has avoided the droning tones of the textbook, and has concentrated on other ways to engage readers, whether through aphorism, anecdote, or a profound, practical involvement that goes beyond criticism as academics know it.[21] Paterson's engagement is both deep and witty. What is on offer in the present four-part trilogy of *Textual Non Sense* aims to redress the balance by providing a much needed complementary shallowness.

---

19   Robert Crawford, *Vestigial Power, Classical Association Presidential Address 2016* (Watford: Classical Association, 2016).

20   In order to spare blushes, this footnote mentions no specific works.

21   See Don Paterson, *The Book of Shadows* (London: Picador, 2004); *The Blind Eye: A Book of Late Advice* (London: Faber and Faber, 2007); *Reading Shakespeare's Sonnets: A New Commentary* (London: Faber and Faber, 2010); *The Poem* (London: Faber and Faber, 2018).

Creative Writing needs to take itself less seriously. Having written *The Modern Poet: Poetry, Academia, and Knowledge since the 1750s*, an all too serious history of poets' frequently spiky relationships with universities and their in-house literary critics, I thought I had better atone now by producing in *Writers' Struggles* a slimmer, sillier companion volume – a wee, subversive, late-born twin.[22] Only the writer who cherishes an instinctive splinter of scepticism about the value of professionalized and academicized Creative Writing teaching can teach Creative Writing well; and, in any case, it's the job of good students to react against undue solemnity in Creative Writing, and to draw inner strength from blowing raspberries at their teachers as well as at some of the writers they hold in highest regard. If the redoubtable Yale Professor Harold Bloom's macho notion of the ever anxious *agon* (thieved in part from Sigmund Freud and T. S. Eliot) lies not too far behind these *Struggles*, then so does a sense that writers young and old need to take themselves at once very seriously and not seriously at all.[23] Writing comes from play as well as from angst, while poetry (not that *Writers' Struggles* is quite poetry) needs play particularly.

Of course (except from grants), most Creative Writers don't make much money, even from teaching Creative Writing,

---

22   Robert Crawford, *The Modern Poet: Poetry, Academia and Knowledge since the 1750s* (Oxford: Oxford University Press, 2001).

23   Harold Bloom, *The Anxiety of Influence: A Theory of Poetry* (New York: Oxford University Press, 1973).

so the third section of the present book, *How to Write a Bestseller in Just 39 Steps*, may serve as a bit of an antidote. It belongs, I suppose, at the more exploitative end of the CW spectrum, the end where courses in newspapers advertise that for only £3000 you can take a 6-hour course with a writer you've barely heard of and emerge as a fully-fledged bestselling novelist. A sort of neo-Edwardian mock-MOOC, the *39 Steps* here might just lead readers and writers to reflect in a sly, refracted way on both the pretentiousness involved in po-faced Creative Writers agonizing over 'the writing process,' and on the continuously vexed relationship between literature and eager commerce. In other words, *How to Write a Bestseller in Just 39 Steps* is attempting to do in a completely lightweight and ludic way something of what Adam Smith may have been up to when in his brilliant Glasgow ruminations he thought not only about literary texts and their production but also about economic and trade productivity in general. If all the textual non sense that follows brings the subjects of literary criticism and Creative Writing right back to their institutional origins as well as shaking them up just a tiny bit in a daft and subversive way, then so much the better. Imagine now a Doctor Adam Smith emoji with a very wide grin and a wink.[24]

No significant work of academic relevance can be written today without a massive grant, and the hyper-institutionalized Professor Mike Foucault is the self-acknowledged Grant Master in this field. Though it may derive in part

---

24   Oh, go on, just one last footnote.

from his now discredited work, *The Nude Criticism*, Professor Foucault's work on what he calls 'bare textuality' has learned from I. A. Richards and his ilk. However, moving far beyond such primitive exemplars, Mike's project engages robustly in the most thoroughgoing and self-reflective way with postmodern textuality, form-filling, networking, and industrial-scale grant capture. Part four of the present volume is given over wholly to Professor Foucault's awe-inspiringly impactful data-harvesting. All aspiring applicants for funding will find in Professor Foucault the perfect mentor, and will have much to learn from his form-filling wisdom as he abolishes the difference between form and forms, text and 'text', grants and *Grandes Écoles*.

PART TWO

Writers' Struggles
A Text Book

with a preface by
William Shakespeare

Preface by William Shakespeare

As the world's consummate literary genius, I have never struggled to produce any of my masterpieces. For all other authors, however, writing is a continuous struggle. In these circumstances, it is surely helpful to draw sustenance, consolation, and inspiration from observing the many struggles that have been faced by writers across the centuries. In this spirit Robert Crawford has compiled the present text bag of texts.

After I stopped working in the theatre (by which time my reputation had traversed the Globe), I was appointed Lord God Professor of Creative Writing at the University of Life's Fife campus where Professor Crawford was then a young lecturer. Over the years, frequently thanks to my generous introductions, he has grown over-familiar with an improbable number of well-known authors, and is now on first-name terms with almost everyone but me. Nevertheless, he has benefited from spending time in my distinguished company, and I have encouraged him repeatedly to take on board some of my own profound classroom interrogations of my creative *praxis*. Not least, I have encouraged him to ponder one of the key questions of the writer's craft: 'What's in a name?'

Attempting to answer this question in the texts that follow, Professor Crawford often reveals that writers are divided selves, compounded of bitterly contending elements, and engaged in an arduous *agon* or creative struggle. Facing up to issues of distraction, destruction, and deconstruction, his thesis that a struggle defines nearly every writer draws at times on his earlier book, *Creative Writing: Aims and Objectives*, but this new work has benefitted immeasurably from a far more profound sense of my own amplitude.

I hope you will find *Writers' Struggle*s rewarding and instructive. It is a volume I recommend to all writers who, like yourself, lack my incomparable gifts.

William Shakespeare,
Centre for William Shakespeare Studies,
The Old Master Building,
School of Literature, Bookmaking, and Creative Writing,
The University of Life,
Fife

The Struggles

SYLVIA STRUGGLED WITH TED TALKS

T. S. STRUGGLED
WITH A FROCK

ROBERT LOUIS STRUGGLED
WITH KIDNAPPING

**Bram struggled
with a bat**

VLADIMIR STRUGGLED
WITH HIS LITTLE LOLLY

DOROTHY L. STRUGGLED
WITH WHIMSY

LAURENCE STRUGGLED
WITH AN OVER-SIZED SHANDY

LAURIE STRUGGLED
WITH ROSÉ AND CIDER

DYLAN STRUGGLED
WITH MILK

MARIO VARGAS STRUGGLED
WITH HIS AUNT

LOUIS STRUGGLED
WITH HIS NEICE

A. A. STRUGGLED
WITH POO

EDGAR ALLAN STRUGGLED
WITH HIS PO

KARL STRUGGLED
WITH POOR MARKS IN GERMAN

**SAMUEL STRUGGLED
WITH HIS DIC**

DANTE STRUGGLED
WITH GETTING LAUGHS

THE BROTHERS STRUGGLED
WITH DEPRESSION

SIMONE STRUGGLED
WITH COMING SECOND

JEAN-PAUL STRUGGLED
WITH NAUSEA

WILFRED STRUGGLED
WITH STRANGE MEETINGS

CHRISTINA STRUGGLED
WITH MARKETING

GERMAINE STRUGGLED WITH CASTRATION ANXIETY

EZRA STRUGGLED WITH HIS PANTOS

ALEXANDER STRUGGLED
WITH A POPE

**HAROLD STRUGGLED
WITH PINTEREST**

MARY STRUGGLED
WITH HER RENAULT

WILLIAM STRUGGLED
WITH HIS MORRIS

FORD MADOX STRUGGLED
WITH HIS FORD

MUNGO STRUGGLED
WITH PARKING

MERVYN STRUGGLED
WITH MOUNTAINEERING

JOHN STRUGGLED
WITH HIS BUNION

AGATHA STRUGGLED
WITH HER STRANGE AFFAIR

CHRISTOPHER MURRAY STRUGGLED
WITH GRIEVING

GERTRUDE STRUGGLED WITH TENDER BUTTONS

SIR KARL STRUGGLED WITH POPPERS

JANE WELSH STRUGGLED
WITH HER LETTERS

CHARLOTTE STRUGGLED
WITH HER PROF

HENRY WADSWORTH STRUGGLED
WITH BODY IMAGE

DAME EDITH STRUGGLED
WITH HER POSTURE

*CHRÉTIEN STRUGGLED
WITH TROILISM*

TENNESSEE STRUGGLED
WITH DESIRE

MURIEL STRUGGLED WITH EDINBURGH'S CRÈME DE LA CRÈME

ELLEN STRUGGLED WITH GLASGOW

THOMAS STRUGGLED
WITH HOBS

J. M. STRUGGLED
WITH A PAN

JANE STRUGGLED
WITH HER P&P

**NORMAN STRUGGLED
WITH A MAILBOX**

J. R. R. STRUGGLED
WITH HIS HABIT

WALT STRUGGLED
WITH GRASS

SAPPHO STRUGGLED
WITH A LIAR

WILLIAM STRUGGLED
WITH A PEN

GEORGE BERNARD STRUGGLED WITH ELOCUTION

BERTOLT STRUGGLED WITH CHALK

DUNCAN BAN STRUGGLED
WITH A CROFT

F. SCOTT STRUGGLED
WITH A MANSION

IAIN STRUGGLED
WITH BANKS

LYTTON STRUGGLED
WITH HIS EMINENCE

WYSTAN STRUGGLED
WITH CLOCKS

MARCEL STRUGGLED
WITH TIMEKEEPING

LORD PHILIP DORMER STAN-HOPE STRUGGLED WITH HIS CHESTERFIELD

SHAMS-UD-DIN MUHAMMAD
STRUGGLED
WITH HIS DIVAN

IRVINE STRUGGLED
WITH HEROINES

JONATHAN STRUGGLED
WITH SPEED

e. e. STRUGGLED
WITH HIS TYPEWRITER

COMPTON STRUGGLED
WITH HIS MAC

EMILY STRUGGLED
WITH HER FEAR OF HEIGHTS

**DON STRUGGLED
WITH HIS LILO**

ANN, CHARLOTTE, AND EMILY
STRUGGLED
WITH THEIR BELLS

ARTHUR CONAN STRUGGLED
WITH CASES

ALDOUS STRUGGLED
WITH THE NEW WORLD

HENRY DAVID STRUGGLED
WITH POND LIFE

GORE STRUGGLED
WITH HIGH SELF-ESTEEM

SØREN STRUGGLED
WITH THE KIRK

CHINUA STRUGGLED
WITH FALLING APART

J.K. STRUGGLED
FOR A SPELL

RABBIE STRUGGLED
WITH THE DIALECT POLICE

SEAMUS STRUGGLED
WITH THE BOG

Immanuel struggled with negativity

FYODOR STRUGGLED WITH AN IDIOT

TOBIAS STRUGGLED
WITH A SMALL E.T.

ANTHONY STRUGGLED
WITH TROLLOPS

GERARD STRUGGLED
WITH MANLINESS

SIGMUND STRUGGLED
WITH <u>EVERY BODY</u>

**TRISTAN STRUGGLED
WITH HIS DADA**

SOMERSET STRUGGLED
WITH HIS MOM

BARBARA STRUGGLED
WITH PIMM'S AND PUBLISHERS

IAN STRUGGLED
WITH HIS SEVENTH AGENT

Julian struggled
with God and Norwich

KARL OVE STRUGGLED
WITH HIS STRUGGLE

EVERYONE STRUGGLES
WITH ENDINGS

Praise for
Writers' Struggles

'This is the book that taught
me everything'
Giovanni Boccaccio

'Touché!'
Gustave Flaubert

'I just can't wait for the
American edition'
Emily Dickinson

Robert, I've proofread up to here, and have managed to get the spacing right (which isn't easy), but am feeling really rather unwell and will have to stop. Please can you proofread from now on? Thanks.   Nigel

That's fine, Nige. Sorry you're a bit under the weather. I think I can get my grad student Flip Rush to handle the rest. R

Thanks, Robert. Just remember to make sure Flip removes all these comments.   Nigel

Of course, Nige. Hope you're on the mend soon! R

Dear Flip,
I wonder if I could ask you to proofread the rest of this? I could arrange payment for you off my research grant: you'd be paid at the university's standard scribal rate, minus the obligatory 65% overheads and a 14% handling charge, but it could be excellent experience for you and might enhance your CV. One thing I'd ask is that you be particularly careful with the spacing in Part 3, for which Lord Tweedsmuir has graciously agreed to supply a preface. I don't want anything to go wrong, especially since he is one of the university's major donors and can be a bit thin-skinned. Please make sure to remove these comments too, so they don't show up in the printed book! Would that be OK? RSVP.
Best, Robert C

Hi Prof. No worries! Flip

PART THREE

How to Write a Bestseller in Just 39 Steps

with a Foreword by

John Buchan,
Lord Tweedsmuil

Foreword by Lord Tweedsmuir

Good evening, Ladies and Gentlemen, and thank you for inviting me. Wherever you may happen to be in the British Empire, it should be easy for you to write a bestseller. This book will make it so.

In my own case, while still a youth at Glasgow University, I wrote to list my profession in *Who's Who* as 'undergraduate', and so in this way I became a bestselling author. This is just the sort of thing one has to do.

It also helps to be someone who understands the way of the world. If I may be permitted once again to draw on my personal experience, I found my stint as Governor General of Canada immeasurably beneficial.

Keep it short. My own experience of writing bestsellers took some time to acquire, but, if you use this book wisely, you can acquire yours in under 39 minutes. Here, drawn up on full display, are all the discipline, drill and veldt-craft necessary for the bestselling author.

Make sure your work reaches Alfred Hitchcock, if you can, and always cash cheques promptly.

Please send my usual speaker's fee, Professor Crawford.

Yours aye,

John Buchan

The Thirty-Nine Steps

STEP 1.

NAME.

In writing a bestseller, it helps hugely to have an established name. Most, though not all, writers find their parents helpful here. Parents tend to be the people who know their children best, and are likely to choose a suitable name that will stand the test of time.

If you are uncertain, or may be misled by having several names, do some research. In 2017 Harvard University's Advanced School of Creative Writing used a digital algorithm along with latitudinal data-mining analysis to develop a programme for optimal authorial nomenclature. The name the computer chose was Dugald.

TITLE.

Some bestselling authors have found it worthwhile to have a title. Byron, whose reputation as 'mad, bad, and dangerous to know' indubitably added to his sales, reaped untold financial, social, and sexual benefits from being a lord. So did Lord Tennyson, who also had Queen Victoria. Queen Victoria had many titles of her own – most notably, perhaps, Empress of India – which helped her in her search to find an agent for her bestselling diaries. Because of the Queen's royal title, however, convention dictated that her agent had to be a secret one. Such behaviour is not generally recommended for untitled people who want to be bestselling writers, because publishers find those sorts of agents offputtingly difficult to contact.

Other titled authors include Sir Walter Scott who, bewilderingly, called all his novels *Waverley*, and often referred to himself as The Great Unknown. This was particularly difficult for his publicist, who begged Sir Walter to stick to his NAME (see Step 1 above), and, after a spectacular bankruptcy, parted company with him, uttering the famous Greek words, ΓΝΩϑΙ ΣΕΑΥΤΟΝ (*know thyself*). It is not essential to know all this in order to write a bestseller, but it may help.

If you do not yet have a title, you have two choices: get one, or refuse one. Notable authors who refused titles are Sir T. S. Eliot and Lord Tom Paine. If you already have a title, you may choose to renounce it (see under **EDITING**, Step 32 below).

STEP 3.

BLOTTING PAPER.

Shakespeare may never have blotted a line, but all other bestselling writers do. Blotting paper is essential if you are going to write a bestseller. Have a large pile on your desk 24/7, and, since you can never be sure at what point inspiration may arrive, always carry a supply about your person.

STEP 4.

AGENTS.

Agents are vital for bestsellers. Ian Fleming, Lee Child, and John Le Carré all have agents. Dr Watson, however, preferred not to be bound to any particular agent, but associated himself with a more general detective agency, Holmes & Hudson. Private detectives can be very useful, especially if you are struggling to find your agent. (see also under **TITLE** at Step 2 above).

STEP 5.

PUBLISHERS

Before you begin to write your bestseller, you must find a publisher. Publishers are advantageous because they will put your **NAME** and **TITLE** in their catalogues, and will contact bookstores to arrange **BOOK-SIGNINGS** (see Step 29). They will also publish an advance summary of your bestseller -- which can be helpful for you to see -- along with blurbs such as 'nail-biting' and 'sensational'. They will encourage you to tweet about the book and give pre-publication interviews. They may even sell film and TV rights. All this will help give structure to your book when you eventually come to write it. As you become more experienced at writing bestsellers, you may find that it pays to write them only after publication.

STEP 6.

PAPER

In this digital age, paper is no longer required to write a bestseller. Just use your imagination.

STEP 7.

FONT

You will need a font. Fonts come in all shapes and sizes and are found not only in great cathedrals and wee parish churches but also in the chapels of stately homes. Fonts have unusual names such as Baskerville, Old Gothic, and Palatino. You must learn all these since they are an essential part of every writer's craft. To hone your craft, test yourself regularly on font names and font recognition (you may find a handy list on a drop-down menu on your computer). As a bestselling author, you will need to christen your book. For more guidance on this, it would be wise to retrace your steps and re-tread Step 1 and Step 2 before proceeding.

STEP 8.

LENGTH

Length is a crucial issue for any bestselling writer. Female authors and even child prodigies are often shorter than male ones, though this rule (while useful as a rough guide) is far from universally true. Before you start to write, and even just after you have begun, your typescript may look very short indeed. However, as the **WRITING PROCESS** develops, you should be confident that it will get longer – unless, of course (and this is unwise), you attempt poetry.

Research suggests that over the last two decades bestsellers have indeed been getting longer. Some of this may be down to improved diet, but the statistics may also have been affected disproportionately by the Harry Potter series, which began about the size of a Ford Anglia but grew as long as a convoy of articulated trucks. Remember the incomparable Max's maxim, Brevity is the soul of wit, and that modern readers avoid the Bible. If your book is still too short, shorten it.

STEP 9.

STATELY HOMES

From *The Mysteries of Udolpho* to *Downtown Abbey*, many bestselling writers have constructed stately homes, abbeys, and romantically ruined castles so vivid that these function not just as locations but as **CHARACTERS** in truly gripping **PLOTS**. Certainly, it is hugely helpful to have somewhere comfortable to write. Is your own home stately enough? If not, don't worry. You can easily find affordable writerly solutions by picking up tips from any number of home-decorating, property, and makeover programmes. These include the popular *Location, Location, Location*, which offers a useful reminder that **LOCATION** (see Step 10a below) remains of paramount importance in bestsellers. Working your way through such a programme, or, better, programmes, is often helpful. They are readily available at any time of day or night, via the very computer on which you do your writing. Many writers, however, prefer to view them on daytime television.

STEP 10.

for the sake of clarity, this Step has been divided into two baby steps:

10a: LOCATION

You can write anywhere.

10b: FLATS

If you do not live in a stately home, but live in an apartment (i.e., what bestselling British writers frequently refer to as a 'flat'), don't worry: you can draw on this location too for atmosphere. At the start of the most celebrated bestselling flat story, a man is skewered by a dagger in his back after arriving unannounced at a London flat and telling the occupant, Richard Hannay, a ridiculous story. This then leads, somewhat indirectly, to 39 steps -- and to this very publication that you are now reading!

Writerly tip: paint your flat white. That way you will be less distracted while writing. Flat whites are favoured by stylish writers. Never, though, confuse a flat white with a white flat. Try to avoid flatness in style.

STEP 11.

THE WRITING PROCESS

This is crucial. Possibly you were taught the writing process at a very young age by someone who called themselves your 'teacher'. Though the received wisdom among many bestselling authors (who themselves teach Creative Writing) is that you must unlearn what you have been taught and begin again, I counsel against all such advice: if you completely unlearn the writing process, you will never be able to write.

THE PSYCHOLOGY OF WRITING

All writers play psychological games with themselves. T. S. Eliot (both before and after he became a bestseller) played patience; Dan Brown sets himself art-historical conundrums; Agatha Christie conducted archaeological digs inside her head. If your game of choice is football, this can be particularly difficult, but is worth trying. Bestselling authors in particular develop their abilities by setting themselves psychological challenges: 'Could Jane Austen have written *Pride and Prejudice* while watching a box-set of *The Simpsons*?' or 'What would happen if I took a chainsaw and slaughtered my extended family?' Such structured challenges involve nuanced aspects of writerly psychology and can free up **THE WRITING PROCESS**. Attempt them regularly, and, as your confidence grows, you may surprise yourself by beginning to deploy them in your practice.

STEP 13.

THE COMPUTER

The computer is a useful tool. This is because it can write books for you.

SLEEP DEPRIVATION

Many bestsellers feature sleep deprivation. Often this is because the protagonist has been captured and is being held at a secret facility, being tortured by dripping water, an electric saw, or the music of Sibelius. Sleep deprivation can be essential to the business of writing. In altered states, the insomniac's brain may become unusually agile, leading to new **PLOTS**, unexpected insights, and astonishing expressions. Over-indulgence in these can be harmful to a bestseller's style, but do make yourself incorporate sleep deprivation into your **WRITING ROUTINE**. Try to practice it for at least twelve hours a day.

STEP 15.

WRITING ROUTINE

Too much panache or polysyndeton is the sworn enemy of bestselling writing. If you ever want to see your books on airport bookstalls, strive as hard as you can to make your writing completely routine.

STEP 16.

THE DEATH OF THE AUTHOR

This is a French technique, given currency by Roland Barthes (1915-1980), and it made him, in a niche market, something of a bestseller among academics. In one sense, it is not worth worrying about because it is inevitable. In another sense, however, it is vital to many bestsellers, being a key feature (if I have understood the book correctly) of *The Murder of Roger Ackroyd*, as well as featuring in altered forms throughout numerous Parisian novels by George Simenon, and also in the work of the late P. D. James. If you want to be a bestselling author, death is useful. Unless you are already very famous, however, do not make the mistake of thinking you can write your books posthumously (for more on this, see Step 22 below).

STEP 17.

SEX

This is also useful to have.

STEP 18.

FAST CARS

Many bestsellers feature fast cars. James Bond has his Aston Martin; Inspector Morse (in the television series, at any rate) has a Jaguar; Miss Marple is the exception, since she usually travels by train. John Buchan may have started the bestseller's love affair with fast cars in *The* (other) *Thirty-Nine Steps*. Occasionally, however, bestselling writers go against this trope: Ann Cleeves's Vera drives a Land Rover. Few poets become best sellers because so many of them can't drive.*

*Never write while driving.

PAGE COUNT

This step (continued on the following page) is quite technical, but important and relatively easy to follow. French scholars recount how an older bestseller, Alexandre Dumas, lost count of the pages of *The Count of Monte Cristo* while counting in Monte Carlo, where he was writing it. Attempting to re-count *The Count*, Dumas discovered that the number of pages altered every so often as he wrote. Notably evident in his manuscript notes and revising, this process proved to be exacerbated in proof during proof-editing; then, as his editors noted, it recurred repeatedly in editing, copy-editing, and post-publication as copies of the book circulated in different revised editions. Part of the cause was **FONT** size (see Step 7 above), which not only varied from edition to edition, but was variously translated into translations as *The Count of Monte Cristo* was published in other languages. Dumas' Count, as the novel recounts, spent a very long time doing time in incarceration, which gave him time to become highly numerate by the second or third volume. Writers' relationships with pages and page counts, though always relative, can become extremely complex, and many are compulsive page counters, whether or not their own page-turners involve pages or counts, which, in the case of the former, all do, but, in the case of the latter, is increasingly rare.

During the late twentieth century many bestselling medical authors, while producing titles such as *Confessions of a Cognitive Neurosurgeon* or *Junior Doctors Amok*, used pagers, but such use was rendered obsolete by the advent of cellphones. If the Count of Monte Cristo had been allowed to have a phone in his cell, neither he nor his author might ever have lost count, thus allowing Alexandre Dumas to write many more bestsellers.

There is no time for further analysis of page counts in a work of this nature. However, it is worth remembering that bestselling diarist Queen Victoria had her own page.

Always number your pages.

STEP 20.

TRANSPORT

As Wordsworth, who was at all times gentlemanly on coaches, so memorably puts it, 'Surprised by joy, impatient as the wind, / I turned to share the transport'. Harry Potter has revived our enthusiasm for old-style coaches, and in our globalized world transport is key to bestsellers. Try to use impressive marque names such as Mercedes, Bentley, and (for older readers) Hispano-Suiza. This will give your bestseller the right tone. Avoid bicycles: readers don't like them, except for motor-bikes. Intercontinental travel by private jet must occur by chapter five at the very latest, or you will lose sales; later chapters may diversify onto sampans, junks, coracles, or hang-gliders. No pedallos.

In bestsellers, chases are a *sine qua non*. Think carefully about how to structure these. If, for example, at the very start of *Goldfinger*, Bond in his Aston had been chasing Goldfinger on his golf-buggy, the whole **PLOT** would have been a foregone conclusion. Effective chases must involve a considerable measure of equality. Chaser and chasee must be evenly matched: two Lamborghinis (the sports cars, not the tractors, since tractors – even if this is clichéd – are notorious for holding up traffic), or perhaps two dromedaries. As your confidence as a writer increases, your protagonist will more and more frequently break the speed limit. Modern bestsellers have a great deal to learn from the bestselling Renaissance courtier-poet Sir Thomas Wyatt: 'They flee from me that sometime did me seek.'

Having a background in transport can be a sure-fire asset to a bestselling author. Captain W. E. Johns, whose bestselling children's novels feature the daredevil air-ace Biggles, was a tugboat captain.

THE AUTHOR:EDITOR RATIO

This is something of a trade secret, but essential to adopt as part of your **WRITING ROUTINE**. If your Author:Editor Ratio remains balanced at precisely 1:1, your writing will never advance. Instead, you will simply edit out every single word that you author. What you need to achieve is Purposeful Authorial Disequilibrium. In essence, this means that the Author component of your Author:Editor Ratio is always at least 0.0001 in excess of the Editor component. If at the very start of your writing day you can use **TIME MANAGEMENT** (Step 30) so efficiently that you manage to accelerate to an A:E R of 3:1, then you will have written at least 3 words.

Inevitably, there will be times when deceleration of A:E R occurs and your Inner Editor will be in the ascendant. Learn to accept this. Some bestselling writers see such moments as opportunities to improve their work, but many fear them. Should you find yourself in a constant state where your A:E R is 7:1, rejoice! You could be the next Alexandre Dumas. If, however, you find your A:E R plunges to 1:7, seek immediate medical assistance. Otherwise, the danger is that you will unwrite all your own books.

STEP 22.

HOW TO WRITE A BESTSELLER WITHOUT EVEN WRITING ONE

In our era when politicians don't write their own speeches, students don't write their own essays, and many people hardly write at all, it is increasingly common for bestselling authors not to write their own bestsellers. This is relatively straightforward if you are a celebrity, a footballer, or a major criminal. These people's bestsellers are often ghost-written (a simple Satanic device); but even if you are not a celebrity, a footballer, or a major criminal, there is another way. You should be aware, however, that this other way normally involves complex legal negotiations (consult your **AGENT** – see Step 4), Estates and Trusts, as well as becoming dead. Nevertheless, this technique has proved popular with such bestselling authors as Arthur Conan Doyle, Ian Fleming, and even Jane Austen, some of whose most recent work was not ghosted but zombied. Further details about this method will be found in Step 16, **THE DEATH OF THE AUTHOR**.

STEP 23.

WRITING WITHOUT READING

This is a method which has found great favour with Creative Writing students, as well as with certain American presidents. Such authors hold that reading is dangerous because it corrupts style and inhibits opinion formation. Similar in some ways to Automatic Writing (see the appendix on 'Surrealist Bestsellers'), this mode of authorship is increasingly practised, and can become a dead-cert route to bestsellerdom.

STEP 24.

WEBSITES

Before you become any sort of author you need to have a website. To become a bestseller, you may need more than one. Websites (formerly known in the trade as 'vanity publishing') are where you provide key statements about your authorial practice. These can be straightforward – 'I AM FAB' – or more sophisticatedly nuanced: 'MY BOOKS ARE PAGE-TURNERS'. They may also feature key tags such as 'NEW YORK TIMES BESTSELLER', though in some circumstances this can lead to legal issues. Include large photographs of yourself and your characters, making clear that they can be reproduced freely under a Creative Commons Licence. Make sure, too, that the left-hand side of your website has a drop-down menu that allows fans to buy merchandize, particularly if your books are pornographic.

Having good bone structure, a recent haircut, and a distinctive website can help you become a bestseller, since increasingly publishers trawl the internet looking at and for authors. In order to make yourself particularly 'discoverable', set up several further websites in the names of other people, each of whom proclaim themselves your Number One Fan. Encourage these fictional admirers to tweet about you.

Don't make the rookie mistake of adding a 'Contact Me' button to your own personal website, and never reveal your email address. Doing so will result in innumerable begging letters, death threats, and requests for guidance about how to write a bestseller. If you *do* receive questions about this last point, simply refer all inquirers to the present publication. Making your contact details public will mean you find out more than you ever want to know about your readers' sex lives, holidays, and eating habits. You will be facebooked and snapchatted to such an extent that your **A:E R** (see Step 21) will plunge immediately into the danger zone.

Always remember, though, to give your contact details to your **AGENT**.

STEP 25.

REPUTATION

In all writing, reputation is crucial, and this is especially so for bestsellers. If you lose your name, you lose everything. You become, quite literally, Anon.

Should you need to recap at this point, if you have lost your name or temporarily forgotten it, simply return now to Step 1, **NAME**, and work again through all the above Steps sequentially until you return to the present Step with a clearer sense of exactly who you are as a writer.

You may wish to repeat this process several times, until you feel wholly comfortable. When you have done so, consider exactly what this may have done for your reputation. All sorts of reputations are available to bestselling writers: John le Carré has something of a reputation as a spy, Ian Rankin has a reputation as a rock musician. Jeffrey Archer also has a reputation. Remember, though, that bestselling writers do not come with any sort of permanent warranty. Once a reputation has been lost or damaged, it may be impossible to restore. This is precisely why each and every writer, long before they become bestselling, should have his or her own personal reputation manager. This person will say things like, 'I think you're in danger of becoming a total dick', or, 'My client's words have been taken entirely out of context.' This person may also burn some of your early books.

STEP 26.

KINDLES

As it used to say in the Latin oath sworn by wannabe readers joining the Bodleian Library in Oxford (a city with a proud history of book-burning): DO NOT KINDLE.

STEP 27.

PLAGIARISM

All bestselling authors plagiarize. Virgil (a bestseller in his time) plagiarized Homer; Dante plagiarized Virgil; Milton plagiarized the lot. As T. S. Eliot put it, 'Immature bestsellers borrow; mature bestsellers plagiarize *Paradise Lost.*'

STEP 28.

UNDERWATER WRITING EXERCISES*

First developed by the bestselling Victorian author Charles
Kingsley, these can be highly effective when used by
Creative Writing groups to develop fluidity and fluency
of style. In continental Europe they were championed by
Jules Verne. They have fallen out of fashion recently, but
were revived for *Jaws*.

*Never practice these exercises unsupervised.

STEP 29.

BOOK-SIGNINGS

Try to sign books by Jilly Cooper. They always sell well.

STEP 30.

TIME MANAGEMENT

Divide your day into two sections: one of these, when you work on your bestselling book, is Aim Time. Some Aims may be small ones, such as a paragraph or a page; others may be larger in scale, such as a trilogy of prequels. These are known respectively as Small Aims and Large Aims. You may find it helpful to break these down into more manageable sections, thus:

Small Aim 1: A Page

Sub-Aim 1.a.1: A Sentence
Sub-Aim 1.a.2: Another Sentence
Sub-Aim 1.a.3: A Third Sentence
and so on.

Often it is worth thinking of individual words as Micro-Aims, and, even in the age of SpellCheck, to be familiar with the Nano-Aim of spelling.

The rest of your day should be spent on Objectives. Objectify your time wisely, using a clock, watch, or other digital device. You can also use alcohol, abusive language, continual prevarication, poor personal hygiene, grandiosity, and sheer bloody-mindedness to make yourself as objectionable as possible.

STEP 31.

PREDESTINATION

If you are predestined to write a bestseller, or even if you simply believe that you are, this can make things easier. To examine whether or not this is the case, examine your computer's pre-set settings, and your own. You may wish to join a cult.

STEP 32.

EDITING

Never read over your own work. To do so will only confuse you. Always remember you are a bestselling author. Reading is strictly for readers.

STEP 33.

YOUR NEXT BOOK

When you are writing a bestselling book, always make sure to talk loudly about what your next book will be about. That will make it easier to finish the book you are currently working on, since you will be increasingly confident that it will be almost nothing in comparison with your next book.

STEP 34.

MONEY

Remember that bestselling books are almost never written in order to make money. Though your **PUBLISHER**, your **AGENT**, and even companies such as Amazon may suggest that your bestselling book will make you incredibly rich, invariably it won't, and you should not believe them. The economics of the book trade have changed enormously in recent years as a result of the dizzying growth in online publishing, digital marketing, bookstore closures, gravitational wave detection, and other complex factors you need not bother your head about. Soon authors will have to pay to be allowed to write at all. At present, though, what you need in order to complete your bestseller is not some unwavering belief that your book will make money. What you need – for printer ink, keyboard batteries, food, and clothing – is simply money itself.

STEP 35.

WORDS

Words are essential for any bestseller. Too many and your book will fail to sell. Too few and it will also fail to sell. As if this wasn't enough, you also need to be careful about which words to use. Be aware that some words can cause offence in certain cultures, and that not all words are nouns.

Most bestselling authors particularly recommend short words, though exceptions should be made for beguiling product placement – 'He sported a huge Heckler and Koch Omnilethamaximizer' – and for many Welsh place-names. As a discipline, try to write a bestseller comprised entirely of words no more than two letters long, except for the exceptions just mentioned. It may help to set this book in Wales.

CHARACTERS

If you are writing for Anglophone readers, avoid using Cyrillic characters. Also Chinese, Arabic, Japanese, Hebrew, Sanskrit, and Greek. All these risk making your bestseller just too expensive to translate for your target market.

STEP 37.

PLOT

Before you start, choose a plot that has not been taken already. Select, too, a headstone with a simple inscription.

Be aware that writing a bestseller, like writing other kinds of book, brings with it dangers of paranoia. You have to keep reminding yourself that not absolutely everything is a plot.

STEP 38.

THE NIELSEN INDEX

It is important to know about and understand the Nielsen Index. This was established by a Danish composer whose music too few people listened to. He sought his revenge by exposing how few books most authors actually sell. The Nielsen Index uses numbers instead of musical notes, and so operates numerically. Its statistics are vital to the publishing industry. **PUBLISHERS** swear by and at them.

The 'Index' aspect of the Nielsen Index means you can look up any book. If your bestseller does not have an index, your publisher may be able to have one constructed either by employing a member of the Society of Indexers, or (less sensitively, but more cheaply) by using an industry algorithm. This helps authors as well as publishers, because it allows each writer to look up his or her own index and find out whether some parts of a particular book are selling better than others. Thus use of the Nielsen Index can be of benefit when selecting and structuring your **PLOT**.

The Nielsen Index can be dispiriting at times. Try to console yourself by strategic use of your **WEBSITES** (return to Step 24).

STEP 39.

CREATIVITY

Not everyone can write a bestseller. You have to accept this. Even if your own book happens to sell badly, you can have the consolation that your sales figures will have assisted other books to climb the **NIELSEN INDEX** and so become bestsellers. In so doing, without doing so directly, you will have helped to create a bestseller.

APPENDIX:
SURREALIST BESTSELLERS

PUBLISHER'S NOTE:

This publication does not have an index.

Praise for
How to Write a Bestseller
in Just 39 Steps

"Having spent decades in poetry,
Robert Crawford is peculiarly qualified
to write this book."
J. K., Edinburgh

"C'est magnifique!"
Alexandre Dumas

"Couldn't have put it better myself."
John Buchan

PART FOUR

Two for the Price of Two

An AHRBCC Big Data Impact
Outreach Critico-Creative
Research Project

Directed by Principal
Investigator Professor
Mike Foucault

Preface by Jo Strive

As Head of Impact and Brand Management at a leading university, I am deeply honoured and appropriate to write the prelude to this work by one of my institution's most widely admired academical practitioners, Professor Mike Foucault, PI. As investigator in a series of high-impact monograph, monotone, and drone outputs, Mike has more than delivered his *Two for the Price of Two* project in ways that have captured the widest and still widening public. In particular, his 24-hour 'lock-in' seminar held at our remote off-campus campus facility saw him working intensively with both co-opted post-postgraduate students and member-of-the-public poets to produce through big data capture and green open-access day-release much of the critical and paratextual 'citizen humanities' work on display herein. After the eventual supervised and unconditional release of the project and its producers, almost all commentators independently sponsored by the university have calibrated the work as 'interesting' and of national research excellence for its research excellence, and this has led to a mini-segment on national television news's *Look North-North-East* current affairs news programme. Unfortunately, due to an unavoidable time-crunch, I am due now at a meeting of the university's Impact Strand Branding Committee, and so must now conclude this all too brief introductionlet, but will now hand over to Mike Foucault's research assistant Kim Statins PhD who will now explain the project's evolutionary methodology. Thank you, and I wish the project every success.

Jo Strive,
Head of Impact and Brand Management

Preface (continued) by Kim Stats

Thank you, Jo. As Jo has explained, my name is Kim Stats, and as well as being Mike's research assistant, he was the supervisor for my PhD on poetic forms. So what I have been asked to do now is to explain some of the forms used in the *Two for the Price of Two* project. These forms were used both by the student participants and by the member-of-the-public poets, and are, in part, the result of Mike Foucault's work on forms in his ground-cutting and truly edge-breaking monograph, *Examine and Control*. In this, his first book (which is also available as an e-book, a downloadable video, and a series of 349 tweets), Mike analysed the forms used by students under examination in the discipline of Practical Criticism, first developed by Ivor A. Richards at the University of Cambridge (not to be confused with Cambridge Analytica) in the 1920s. In *Two for the Price of Two*, as well as handing these forms to students, we also handed them to poets. Not all of the students were told they were students, and not all of the poets were told they were poets; nor were either or both groups told what to do with the forms, though it was understood that poetry would be involved. This meant that some of the students believed themselves to be poets, and some of the poets believed themselves to be students, and many believed themselves to be both both and neither. This means that participants acted simultaneously as poet, critic, and poet-critic, going both beyond criticism and beyond poetry through taking part in the new, hybrid discipline often called 'Creaticism' but sometimes known too as 'Critive Writing'.

Having constructed through the above procedures what Mike Foucault has designated 'a zone of productive situational ambiguity', all participants were then told to act as if under exam conditions and were seated at numbered desks. In the following pages all participants have been anonymized and named after the number on their desks. Data gathered from the forms has been formally registered as gathered data and therefore is subject to data protection protocols except where data has been lost or sold on in breach of university regulations. This lost data will be published in an appendix which, as yet, has been left empty for the purpose, but all the other data can be found on the forms themselves. For formal purposes, the forms were divided thus:

Title
Name
Date
Number
Address
Genre
Analysis

My own analysis of participants' forms reveals revealing differences in creative-critical approach, and draws also on differences in my own critical-creative practice. It can be summarised as follows:

Title In this section many participants wrote the title of what they believed was the text on which they were being examined. Thus, participant 347 (whose text was the word 'MITHACA') wrote 'MITHACA' in the title section. Other participants chose to interpret this section in terms of literary works alluded to. Thus participant 23 (whose text was also the word 'MITHACA'), wrote '*The Odyssey*' in the *Title* section, while participant 98 wrote 'C. P. Cavafy's "Ithaca"'— presumably a reference to the poem 'Ithaca' by the poet C. P. Cavafy. Other participants, unsure what the title might be, simply guessed at one. Participant 764 wrote 'Ode to Autumn'; participant 562 wrote '*The Waste Land*'; while participant 2 wrote 'Maybe a Shakespearean Sonnet?'. Many participants supplied under Title the title of the critical essay that they went on to write: examples of this included 'The Trope of *Nostos* in Homeric Epic and in Contemporary Poetry', 'Error's Wandering Way', and 'My Essay'. Other participants (following a practice which Mike Foucault has sometimes designated 'self-referential presentation') wrote in the *Title* section words such as 'Ms', 'Mrs' or 'Dr'. Four participants, perhaps self-selected from among our university's *jeunesse dorée*, wrote 'Lord' or 'Right Honourable.' One participant (number 41, of whom more later), wrote in crayon 'Big Yin'.

Name This section gave rise to considerable misunderstanding. Fourteen candidates wrote 'William Shakespeare', seven wrote 'Homer', and one (perhaps in error) wrote 'Mike Foucault'. Participant 764 (see above), having written 'Ode to Autumn' in the *Title* section, also wrote 'Ode to Autumn' in the *Name* section. Many participants seem to have thought they were being invited to name the text in front of them (which was presented without a title) and so produced such contributions as 'Paradise Isle', 'Ode to Golf', and 'Arnold'. Where participants appear to have written their own names in this section, these have been removed in order to preserve strict anonymity. One participant wrote, 'Why are we being asked to write our names in what Professor Foucault's book assures its readers will be a strictly anonymous exercise?' Participant 41 wrote in this section the words 'I cannae remember.'

Date In this section the participant who wrote 'William Shakespeare' wrote 'circa 1603'. Several participants wrote 'It has proved impossible to date exactly the origins of *The Odyssey*.' Participant 465 wrote, 'I have a date allergy and so will not fill in this section', while most participants wrote the date of the day on which they were completing the form, with one participant adding, 'It seems later', and another appending the words 'April is the cruellest month.' Participant 720 wrote 'Are you asking?'. Participant 721 wrote, 'I think I should say here and now that I am married.' Participant 722 wrote, 'I would not date Professor Foucault if he were the last man on earth.' Participant 41 wrote in crayon, 'Aye, sure.'

Number This section drew from participant 653 a nuanced, fifteen-page essay on 'Number and Metre in Caroline Verse'. This work is too long to reproduce here, and was marked down by Professor Foucault on the grounds that the word 'Caroline' was admissible only in the section designated *Name* and so was wholly inadmissible under *Number*. Several participants wrote down the longest number they could think of, and one even used a decimal point. Many participants wrote down the number in front of them on their desk. One participant wrote, 'I can remember the name of T. S. Eliot's street but not the number' (which Professor Foucault thought confusing – and a possible 'category error' – because of the use of the word 'name'); another participant wrote, 'Legion'; and a further participant wrote 'Thirteen Ways of Looking at a Blackbird', but could not remember the twelfth. Participant 41 wrote 'I hae lost the will tae live and ma seat at this desk is sae hard that ma bum is getting number and number.'

Address This section prompted many participants to attempt to reproduce in the text box Robert Burns's 'Address to the Deil', 'Address of Beelzebub', 'Address to Edinburgh', or 'Address to the Unco Guid, or the Rigidly Righteous', while others (perhaps interpreting the prompt more liberally) wrote out all of 'To a Louse', 'To a Mouse', or 'To a Haggis'. Participant 379 addressed Professor Mike Foucault directly in a witty pastiche of 'To a Mouse', whose first line followed the original first line word for word, except that it substituted the word 'Big' for the word 'Wee'; Professor Foucault, however, insisted that this participant's work was inadmissible since the university's anti-plagiarism software had identified it as 87% unoriginal and so it should be treated as plagiarism and excluded from the sample. I have kept it in a special drawer. Other participants chose to address a variety of world leaders, major companies, and university figures in a lively variety of (occasionally questionable) freeform text which has been redacted for purpose of statistical analysis and for legal reasons; most participants, however, wrote their own postal addresses, which cannot be quoted here for reasons of data protection legislation, but which I have also kept in a locked, password-protected drawer. In the **Address** section one participant wrote 'No. Trouser suit.' Participant 41 wrote 'University of [I have redacted a word here KS], Alcatraz Hall of Residence.'

Genre Though one participant provided a full and thoughtful account of the evolution of the epic poem from Classical times through the Renaissance epics of Tasso, Ariosto, and Milton to contemporary variations by Derek Walcott and Les Murray, most participants wrote either 'Male' or

'Female', though several complained that this section was offensive and unnecessary. Participants 53 and 865 wrote (apparently independently of each other) 'Mike Foucault needs Diversity Training'. Participant 41 wrote simply, 'Aye'. Participant 9 produced a dissertation that argued the need to view the creative as a variation on the critical and the critical as a variation on the creative, so that in future all textuality should be regarded in terms of creato-critical or criticreative hybridization, even when presented through post-Raymond Williams keywords or post-Wimsattian verbal iconography inflected by the sculptural and collaborative poetics of Ian Hamilton Finlay. Professor Mike Foucault particularly praised this response and is now co-authoring a monograph, *Two for the Price of Two*, with this participant, who cannot be named here for data protection reasons and whose name (for similar reasons) will nowhere appear in the published monograph.

Analysis Since some of the participants' analyses are quoted in the pages that follow, only short extracts from participants' responses will be given here. Participant 872, in a particularly abusive response (which I present in redacted form) wrote 'SEND THAT ****** MIKE ****AULT FOR ******* ANALYSIS NOW!' Participant 69 wrote, 'Since I am myself undergoing analysis during this period, it would be inappropriate for me to comment here though I would dearly like to do so.' Participant 421 wrote, 'As a fully qualified Jungian analyst, I must say that I believe Professor Foucault's research methodology is predicated upon mistaken principles. In addition, I would like to ask how much longer we will be kept here without food.' Participant 900 wrote, 'I resent being asked for an intimate account of my sex life', and went on to write a largely biographical account of the student years of Allen Ginsberg. Participant 12 simply quoted from Professor Foucault's *Examine and Control*: 'All so-called literary analysis, unless it represents a new and paradigmatic creative misprision, merely constitutes a further attempt at the institutionalization of systemic incarceration within the commodified prison-house of language' (p358). Participant 103 wrote, 'As a trained paper-maker and chemical analyst (BSc and MSc, Chemistry, Durham, 1996), even without my laboratory, I believe this substance on which I am writing to be Hahnemühle matt fine art photo rag 308gsm'. Participant 41 wrote 'Whisky'.

Thus concludes my analysis of participants' responses to this wonderful project. If you would like to contact me for further details, please do email me at

kstats@knowledgetransferandculturalimpactfacultycrosssectoralgrouphqannexe.ac.uk

or write to me, Dr Kim Stats, Portakabin 7, Research Assistants Block, Grounds of the Mike Foucault Annexe, Core Impact Building, Data Analysis Quadrant, The Digital Humanities Science Park, Cross-Sectoral Campus, Fundholders' Drive, UniLab 9.

Kim Stats

Funder's Foreword by Sir John Stallholder

As Chair and Chancellor of the Arts and Humanities Research Bureau Corporation Constellation (AHRBCC), which funded Professor Mike Foucault PI's wonderful project, *Two for the Price of Two*, I would like to remind all stakeholders that the AHRBCC's mission now and going forward is not to fund fuddy-duddy and regressive research of the old, medievalizing write-a-book sort, but instead to plough millions into edge-cutting collaborative projects involving large teams, large team-members, as much big data as possible in order to maximize input, costs, overheads, and projects' projected cross-sectoral and interdisciplinary impact on the economy and society. Though this is not the place to repeat the essential funding findings of our three recent, downloadable large-scale, cross-cutting reports, *The Value and Culture of the Arts, The Culture of the Arts and Value*, and *The Arts of Culture and Value*, nevertheless I choose to mention them here as examples of the value of our work in culture and the arts across the monetized university sector, the creative industries, and far beyond.

Suffice it to say that we must remain at all times vigilant and complacent in all our dealings with government, industry, and external users. We must strive for excellence, impact, and outreach. We must demonstrate to society at large, to our newly monetized private and public universities, and, not least, to ourselves the private-public funders at all times transparent money for value and the arts. Though I need to leave soon for a colloquium of key players at a symposium in a major central Manhattan hotel, I do wish to single out three of the most remarkable aspects of Professor Foucault's wonderful project. Firstly, its girth and ambition: seldom have so many participants had their data crunched in so many ways to produce such economy: the sheer scale of the work itself demonstrates the benefit of economies of scale to our economy, particularly given its overall scale. Secondly, I commend to you the light-touch yet remarkable impact of this research, which has resulted not only in the mini-segment on national television news's *Look North-North-East* current affairs news programme to which Jo Striving has referred, but also in the astonishing impact of the website created by the assistant research assistant's assistant, John Oak. This is surely the first time that an AHRBCC knowledge-transfer worker has had a tree named after him. So, all in all, I cannot praise too highly this wonderful and strictly audited project whose forms alone, if laid end to end, would reach between here and I. A. Richards. None of us can predict just how far the resulting impact of this AHRBCC grant funding will reach, but let us hope that such a project of hybrid creaticism and critivity may even produce the next Professor Mike Foucault – or even perhaps the next J. F. K. Rowling!

Sir John Smallholder,
Chair and Chancellor of the Arts and Humanities Research
Bureau Corporation Constellation,
Light-Touch House,
Powerbase Court,
Lobbying,
Sussex

Methodological Prolegomenon by Sally Data

Though much of my work has been on cognitive divergence, the economy of the brain, and neural pathfinding, I was delighted when my recently digitized colleague Mike Foucault invited me to be paid off his grant for the wonderful project *Two for the Price of Two* and to handle the financial, data-intensive and techno-ethical aspects of the project for an outlay of over £1.5M. In developing the project's methodological interface and corpus-analytical critico-cortexical software, I have throughout borne this figure in mind and have made use of the latest edge-cutting digital hardware as well as of my own family members. Throughout, going forward, our aim has been to move from big data analysis to scanty results that can be easily understood by the public after experts have explained the results to them. With this in mind, throughout we have deployed parallel programming of critico-creative corpora materials, allowing these to interact with each other and, in turn, to interact maximally with each other's end-users as the project progresses. To give a specific example, deploying a corpus-driven, text-analysis methodology using big data frameworks, the team (57 members, including myself) has scanned and analysed the complete plays of William Shakespeare and subjected the lexical items therein to a process of digital honing, anagramatization and typographical reconfiguration to produce the resulting meta-text which appears on page 183 of this book along with a selection of participants' analyses of the resulting work. Similar methodologies have been operative in generating other texts within the project, and these have been subject to intensive financial, psycho-ethical, and retro-innovative scrutiny. All participants have been thoroughly indoctrinated in the AHRBCC's *Ethical Code of Conduct for Sustainability and Resilience in Cognitive Assessment in Cultural Value in the Arts and Humanities Creative/Critical Industries Strategic Project Assessment*, and have been thoroughly vetted to make sure that none of them are vets. I have extreme confidence in the robustness of the methodology employed and in all relevant remuneration, and I hope you too will profit from the work that follows.

Sally Data,
Research Fellow and (for tax purposes)
Independent Consultant,
Trough,
Kent

Technical Appendix

A technical appendix, detailing all the hardware and software used, along with full details of the code, participants' addresses, telephone numbers, and other details will be found on the project website as soon as it is available, and will be available for sale to bona fide political parties. A further massive grant has been applied for in connection with this work.

In the following pages of *Two for the Price of Two* the creative work is generally presented in large bold type and a selection of the participants' responses is presented below, though in the online version Professor Mike Foucault contests what he calls 'this absurd binary division'. His arguments about the matter are currently the subject of a judicial review.

Two for the Price of Two

Bringing together creative work and criticism in a project that is both doubly rich and doubly funded, *Two for the Price of Two* draws on creative writing pedagogy, critical commentary, and slits of the tongue to move beyond criticism to a new shared intellectual space. I hope that this forked-tongued work will provoke in readers exactly that sense of 'wild surmise' first experienced by the great Romantic traveller and poet John Keats on his visit to Scotland.

Mike Foucault

Much have I travelled in the realms of golf
    And many grand estates and courses seen;
    Round many western islands have I been
Where caddies rescue clients from the rough.
Oft in a book I took down from the shelf
    I read of bunkers in a green demesne;
    Yet did I never breathe its pure serene
Till I heard shouts beside the North Sea surf:
Then felt I like some watcher of the skies
    When a new planet swims into his ken;
Or like stout Cortez when with eagle eyes
    He saw the fairways shine – and all his men
Looked at each other with a wild surmise –
    A golf ball on a peak in Darien.

John Keats

FIRS AMONG EQUALS

Participant 41: 'Viewed through the prism o ecocriticism, this piece appears a celebration o the egalitarian spirit o the forests o ma native land.'

Participant 749: 'Possibly an allusion to R. M. Ballantyne's *Adventures in the Fir Trade*.'

LITTLE-READ BOOK

Participant 901: 'This probably refers to Milton's Latin poetry.'
Participant 86: 'This is a piece of counter-revolutionary propaganda by an anti-Maoist revisionist.'
Participant 41: 'Sounds tae me like Mike Foucault's *Examine and Control*.'

SEM TEXT

Participant 77: 'This references the explosive potential of social media and the way in which weaponized discourse has permeated the fabric of all advanced capitalist societies.'
Participant 503: 'Should this read "SEND TEXT"?'

OXFROD

Participant 127: 'This work is a savage indictment of the English class system which sends its chosen few to elite fee-paying schools, then to study at an elite ancient university, and then from there they progress to running the country with their old chums.'

Participant 846: 'I laughed until I cried. I applied for a Masters degree there. It only lasted 8 months because they wanted to put us out so they could accommodate more lucrative summer schools in the college.'

Participant 2: 'All that glisters is not gold. Great place for a holiday, though.'

NANNIA

Participant 362: 'This is a witty illusion to C. S. Elliot.'
Participant 740: 'Perhaps deriving from the work of Sir Karl Popper, this piece critiques the "nanny state" and can be aligned with neo-liberalism.'
Participant 49: 'Reminds me of J. M. Barrie.'

FORGET-ME-NOTE

Participant 697: 'I know just what this feels like.'

Participant 12: 'This has a rich, plangent timbre, heightened by judicious use of hyphens which enhance the innate musicality of the phrasing. The rejected lover sounds a note of profound melancholy.'

Participant 917: 'Is it to do with a flower?'

GATHER YER ROSEBUDS
WHILE YE MAY

Participant 41: 'I ken this weel as an auld Scots sang.'

Participant 564: 'This is a lyric by Robert Herrick, the Yorkshire vet, and is probably addressed to someone in a farmyard.'

Participant 459: 'The insistent note of *carpe diem* is unmistakable, and is rendered more intense by the Glaswegian intonation.'

MY LOVE IS LIKE A
RED RED SORE

Participant 41: 'I ken this weel as an auld Scots sang.'
Participant 387: 'Read from the standpoint of the medical humanities, this intense lyric cry is a lament for lost sexual freedom in an age when surgery was less advanced. It may date from the eighteenth century.'

STARTWARS

Participant 41: 'Aye, bring it oan.'

Participant 349: 'This piece speaks to a post-Baudrillardi-an readership for whom mass culture is inevitably part and parcel of the militarized state. Collapsing 'force' and 'the force', it elides the commodification culture of Hollywood merchandizing with the relentless appetite of Trump/Putin/Xi-era capitalism for conflict.'

SLAUGHTER
IS
THE
BEST
MEDICINE

Participant 387: 'Again, read from the standpoint of the medical humanities, this is a particularly disturbing work.'
Participant 2: 'This simply does not make sense, unless one takes an invasively Malthusian approach.'

WAR'S
OWN

Participant 887: 'Succinctly and effectively, this piece expresses the 'band of brothers' feeling of intense comradeship felt between fighting men.'

Participant 56: 'As a feminist, I think this is a satire on the widely-read twentieth-century magazine *Woman's Own*.'

IN THE LIE OF DUTY

Participant 348: 'This clearly alludes to Wilfred Owen's presentation of Horace's line as "The old lie, *Dulce et decorum est pro patria mori*".'

Participant 854: 'This clearly alludes to the Clint Eastwood movie.'

LET US BRAY

Participant 560: 'This may be a reference to upper-class English leaders such as Boris Johnson, or else to President Trump.'
Participant 462: 'It is hard to tell whether this represents anti-religious satire, or a longing for transcendental communication in a secular era.'
Participant 821: 'Obviously alludes to the eponymous Vicar.'

DAS KRAPITAL

Participant 19: 'Punning both on the title of Karl Marx's magnum opus and on the name of the Krupp munition works, this work shows the inter-relationship of capital and militarism in nineteenth-century society.'

Participant 864: 'This is a quotation from Samuel Beckett.'

WRECK LESS

Participant 239: 'This work records the ecological anxiety felt by many in our time and first voiced by Robert Burns in his "To a Mouse", when he writes "I'm truly sorry man's dominion / Has broken nature's social union." Later, Heidegger said much the same sort of thing about dogs.'

Participant 974: 'This is a protest against domestic violence, and reminiscent of a lost work by Sylvia Path."

MY MIS-SPELT YOUTH

Participant 686: 'Suffused with nostalgia for the poet's early years when she was being taught to write by a strict creative writing teacher, this work laments lost opportunities – possibly in publishing or proofreading.'

Participant 43: 'Could this be an allusion to that ancient wholegrain, "spelt wheat"?'

MITHACA

Participant 375: 'This is a pet name for 'Myth Kitty', which is what the poet Philip Larkin called his cat.'

Participant 438: 'Summing up the whole of Western culture, particularly phallocentric and heteronormative Western culture, the work here presents through typographical intervention a withering critique of the impulse towards the false consolation of the 'return home' as imagined by the male imaginary, and as feared by the female imaginary as figured in the figure of Lady Penelope.'

INDIA'S JAIN AUSTEN

Participant 47: 'This text invites a postcolonial reading that invokes Bhabha and Spivak. Presenting Austen as "other", its signification lies in its readiness to move beyond the "universally acknowledged" mercantile truths of Christianity. By taking a cross-cultural, interfaith stance, it problematizes statements of absolute belief.'

Participant 379: 'Surely this is a spelling error. Jane Austin is not a car.'

DRECONSTRUCTION

Participant 840: 'Setting creative writing against the post-structuralist thought of Jack Derrida is a false dichotomy. As Mike Fucault has shown in his book, all writing contains the seeds of its own destruction deep within the creative process and deserves a grant to be investigated more deeply.'

Participant 341: 'This verbal icon emblematizes Kristevan dread of the abyss.'

BROADBARD

Participant 97: 'In Gaelic culture the figure of the bard is sometimes depicted as an old fat guy, but seldom as a broad. The text here presents a transgressive and transgender figure of the poet, reminiscent of Virginia Woolf's notion of creative androgyny, which may also be considered critically.'
Participant 147: 'Neither William Shakespeare nor Robert Burns owned a computer.'

ALWAYS
SHAKE
SPEAR

Participant 16: 'By questioning the apparently unchanging place of Shakespeare in the literary canon, the poet here helps to make room for himself.'
Participant 811: 'This reminds me of processed foods. Also of conflict.'

CREATIVE
WRITING
WORKSOP

Participant 549: 'I have met many such people. They are the bane of literature, and should not be allowed to take the course.'

Participant 856: 'This text problematizes the very notion of creative writing teaching, asking the perennial question, "Can Poesy Be Taught?", but also answering it in its own idiosyncratic way with an assertion of pedagogical authority, albeit laced with a tincture of subversion.'

ABSOLUTE CARLESSNESS

Participant 547: 'The writer presents an ecological idyll of Theocritean simplicity without denying a sense of all-pervasive (post)modernity.'

Participant 41: 'This is yon auld truism that loadsa poets cannae drive.'

THE
WIDE
WORD
WEB

Participant 418: 'The writer would achieve a more impressive effect if the spacing between the letters was increased.'
Participant 67: 'Perfect description of the prose of Sir John Stallholder.'

EIN STEIN

Participant 12: 'The prose here possesses a lapidary simplicity.'
Participant 764: 'I do not know German.'

WINTER
TAKES
ALL

Participant 556: 'Probably an allusion to Shakespeare's *A Midsummer Night's Dream*.'
Participant 97: 'Probably an allusion to winter.'

I CON

Participant 41: 'Reads like the subtitle o the autobiography o Professor Mike Foucault.'

Participant 384: 'A subtle and witty allusion to the Cold War stand-off between W. K. Wimsatt's influential literary-critical work *The Verbal Icon* and the non-verbal iconography of the Russian Orthodox Church.'

PINE FOR REST

Participant 987: 'I believe this translates a phrase from Goethe's 1774 epistolary novel *The Sorrows of Young Werther*, though the trope of forest longing is more widespread in Germanic Romantic art, music, and literature.'
Participant 41: 'Me tae.'

THE NIGHT AT THE END
OF THE TUNNEL

Participant 763: 'In Sir Thomas Malory's *Le Morte d' Arthur* the Knight at the End of the Tunnel is one of Guinevere's lovers.'
Participant 246: 'This reminds me of a lecture by Jo Strive.'

GODBYE

Participant 17: 'This reminds me of Alasdair Gray.'
Participant 569: 'This reminds me of God.'
Participant 479: 'This reminds me of my Mum.'

About the contributors

John Buchan (aka Lord Tweedsmuir) has worked in fiction, biography, autobiography, politics, history, and propaganda. He has also worked in the army, British and colonial government, publishing, and academia. He was voted Oxfordshire Pipe-smoker of the Year in 1926.

Robert Crawford's eight full collections of poetry include *The Scottish Ambassador* (Cape, 2018). He was Professor of Modern Scottish Literature and Bishop Wardlaw Professor of Poetry at the University of St Andrews, until retired at gunpoint.

Sally Data began her career in Boring, Wyoming, before being promoted to Professor in the Department of Transparency at Labyrinth College. For many years she has worked (for tax purposes) as an Independent Consultant. Her clients include the AHRBCC, Bodmin Moor School of Munitions, and Professor Mike Foucault.

Mike Foucault is author of the edge-cutting monograph, *Examine and Control* (Labyrinth College Press, 2006) and has several offices. In 2015 he was awarded the AHRBCC's largest ever grant, as well as a personal chair, a Lifetime Research Fellowship, and two Mercedes limousines. He is married to the philanthropist Iona Bighouse.

John Keats works in the Medical Humanities.

William Shakespeare is a freelance poet and dramatist.

Sir John Stallholder enjoyed a long and lucrative career as a non-executive director with some of the world's leading companies, including Lehman Brothers, Royal Bank of Scotland, Carillion, and Toys R Us, before being appointed to lead an HM Government review of UK higher education funding, *Privatising Knowledge for Value in Culture and the Arts*. Knighted for his services to service, he has served as Chair and Chancellor of the Arts and Humanities Research Bureau Corporation Constellation since 2010.

Kim Stats wrote a doctorate on Advanced Data Manipulation under the supervision of Professor Mike Foucault. Kim now works as his Research Assistant. She lives with her Mum.

Jo Strive and her partner, Major Grant Capture, run a private military academy on Bodmin Moor. Jo also works in the arms trade and as Head of Impact and Brand Management for several competing universities. She travels a lot for work and pleasure, and is writing a book about attack dogs.

Index Index

Textual Non Sense
By Robert Crawford

First published in this edition by Boiler House Press, 2021
Part of UEA Publishing Project
Copyright © Robert Crawford, 2021

Cover Design and Typesetting by Louise Aspinall
Photo by Aisha Farr
Typeset in Arnhem Pro
Printed by Tallinn Book Printers
Distributed by NBN International

ISBN: 978-1-911343-78-3